Bouba & Zaza
respect water

Zaza sat in the yard drawing figures in the sand. Her mother said to her: "Zaza, I am just going to the market to get some mangoes and fish. Don't do anything naughty, I'm coming straight back."

It was very hot and Zaza was thirsty. She went up to the barrel that was used to catch rain water. The little girl picked up the bucket that was next to it, filled it with water, and drank… and drank… and drank… all the water in the bucket!
When her mother came back she found her little girl playing.
"You were a good girl, Zaza, well done. I am going to prepare the meal."

Two hours later, Zaza started crying and holding her tummy.
"What's the matter, Zaza, why are you crying?"
"My tummy hurts Mummy, my tummy really hurts."
"You must be hungry, my Zazou. Food is nearly ready."
"I'm not hungry, I am going to be sick," said Zaza, bending over in pain.

Zaza did not usually complain. She was not like her brother Abdou who was always moaning over nothing. So her mother was worried.

"It's very hot and you have not drunk anything since this morning. Quick, drink this glass of water."

"I'm not thirsty. I was drinking all morning."

"What did you drink? The jug in the kitchen is full."

"I drank water from the yard, the water from the barrel!"

"Zaza, that water is not good to drink. It's not drinking water! You know that. Quick, we must go and see the doctor at the health clinic. He will make you better."
It was very difficult for Zaza to walk. She had to stop all along the road to throw up. In front of the health clinic there was a long queue. But everyone let Zaza go first.

"Well, Zaza, what happened?" the doctor asked.
"I… I… I drank a bucket full of water but that water was not good to drink!" she replied, sobbing.
The doctor understood straight away what was wrong. He gave the little girl some medicine.
"I hope you will never do it again," the doctor said to her. "Quickly go and rest, and don't forget to drink a lot before you go to bed, but drinking water this time!"

On the way home, Zaza murmured: "I never want to drink water again. I hate water. Water is dangerous."
She came across Bouba, who had just finished playing a game of football with his friends.
"I heard you were sick. Is it serious?" asked Bouba.
Zaza took the glass he had in his hand and threw it away.
"Stop it! What are you doing? I'm thirsty!"
"Don't drink it. Do you want to get sick like me?"

"Zaza, you are talking nonsense," said her mother. "Water is bad for your health if it is not drinking water. But water lets us live. Without water we could not do anything!"
"But water made me ill! And also, Bouba nearly drowned the other day in the sea, didn't you Bouba, so it's true… And Auntie's house was flooded when the big rains came! Hey Bouba, it is true… I hate water. And I don't need it!"

Zaza's mother smiled.
"You have to eat a little something. What would you like?"
"Tonight I would like to eat some grilled fish!"
"Oh, did you forget that fish live in water?"

"Oh, well, a little cassava then, but that's all!"
"Cassava needs water to grow," her mother said, laughing. "And didn't you know that I need water to cook it? And the bowl that you will use, do you think I wash it with earth?"
"Oh, well, I won't eat then. It doesn't matter, I'm not hungry."
"OK then, but tomorrow, once you are better, maybe you will change your mind…" said Bouba cheekily.

"Do you want to go straight to bed then?"
"Yes, I just want to wash and that's all!"
"And what are you going to wash with, my little Zazoubidou?" said Mummy, laughing.
"With soap!"
"And what will you rinse it off with?"
"With… with nothing at all. I'm going to bed without washing. I will slip on my nice nightdress and…"
"It won't stay nice very long, Zazou! I wanted to wash it tomorrow but if you hate water you will just have to wear it dirty!"

Zaza began to think. She looked at Bouba, who was also smiling more and more. Well, her mother was probably right but she did not want to admit it, so she continued:
"Too bad, I will wear it dirty!"
And because she still had a tummy ache, Zaza went off to the end of the yard.
"Don't forget to empty a bucket of water in the toilet," said Mum.
"Of course, Mum, I always do!"
Zaza's mother and Bouba burst into laughter. The little girl laughed too, for she understood the lesson.

"I was angry, Mum. I know I was wrong to drink that water! I should have drunk the filtered water that you left in the jug. I know that water is life."

"And what's more Zaza, water is pretty – it is light, it flows, it moves," added Bouba. "Look at the sea, it changes colour: blue, green, grey, turquoise. And when it is clear, you can even see yourself in it.

It's magical!"

"Do you think you are a poet today?"
said Zaza, a little upset.
"Zaza, be nice to Bouba! Bouba, the sea
is beautiful, but it is under threat. Men treat
it badly: they pour their dirty water into it,
and toxic liquids from factories
– all sorts of things!
The fight against this pollution
is very difficult, because what
is at the bottom of the sea,
or dilutes in water,
is often invisible."

"Zaza, water is precious. Each one of us must be responsible. You should not waste it when you play, or leave taps on. You know just how useful it is!"

"That's true, Mum, I will be careful. I won't play any more water games with Bouba. Now we will play soccer! It is true and I will tell my story to everyone at school tomorrow."

"Really tell everything?" said Bouba, laughing.

"Hey Bouba, instead of mocking me you could go and get me a glass of water please! It's good for your health!"

Illustrations: Thomas Penin

© UNESCO and Michel Lafon Éducation, 2011